Broken But Not In Pieces

BY

Monica J. Brazell

For permissions or inquiries, contact:
[Monica Brazell] MonicaJ0933@yahoo.com

ISBN: 979-8-218-75985-8

Printed in the United States of America
First Edition, 2025

Disclaimer

This book contains content intended for mature readers. The names in this book may or may not be accurate, the Author nor the Publisher will be held liable for any damage or untruth with the literacy of this book. This book is from one's personal life experiences or advice to readers to gleam from one's perspective.

Contents

4 ·

Dedication

First, I dedicate this book to God, the head of my life — for giving me the strength to speak my truth, for walking with me through my darkest moments, and for never letting go of my hand when I was ready to give up.

To my grandparents, Peter & Lula B. Jones — thank you for being the example of what true love and faithfulness looks like. Your legacy of strength and devotion lives in me.

To my spiritual mother, Terry Nathaniel — thank you for walking with me through this season of my life. Thank you for staying up with me until 3 a.m., for speaking life over me, and for never allowing me to give up on God or myself. To every person who prayed for me — your prayers covered me when I didn't have the strength to pray for myself. I am forever grateful.

To my children, Tyronda Dabney, Tony Bell, Jasmine Jones and Jeremy Bradley, and my grandchildren, Major Bell and Amaire Bell — Last but not least, even **though,** much of the pain I've endured came through my Husband, Jeremy Brazell, I cannot write this book without including his name in this dedication. Through it all, he believed in me even when I didn't believe in myself. He saw something in me that

I couldn't see, and when God placed it on his heart to open JJ'S Soul Food at 3156 Chelsea Ave, Memphis TN 38108, he invested in that vision and in me. That step of faith brought the best out of me, for that, I am truly grateful. I want to publicly thank you, Mr. Brazell for believing in me and I humbly apologize for waiting so long to say it.

I pray this book becomes a guide for everyone. When life gets hard, when love feels confusing, and when your heart needs direction — may these words remind you to always turn to God.

This book was birthed out of pain — but it lives because of purpose.

With love,
Monica J. Brazell

Foreword Points

The dolefulness in your first chapter was palpable. Silence is not a sign of weakness; it's a sign of maturity. Obedience is better than sacrifice! Obedience demonstrates a trusting relationship with God, a willingness to follow His guidance and a recognition of His sovereignty. Jehovah desires our obedience from the heart, not just outward actions. You showed yourself as a true woman of God, by obeying His word. "Peace not Pieces, I am so proud of you, I love you for life!"

SISTER ANGELA KELLY

*The **very** first chapter grabbed my heart, soul, and spirit. It was birth out of obedience to God. It speaks volumes of truths, things I personally knew, some I didn't know. This truth, with God's anointing will bear fruits of the spirit. This book will help women and men to become free and stay free from chains that try to keep **them** in bondage and destroy **them**. Thank God for the strength and perseverance he gave her to endure being broke but not in pieces. Love always your*

GOD MOTHER ROBBIE JONES

This book gives a voice to women suffering silently in the marriages. Let it be a light to you as a God fearing woman to take the journey with Him (God) as your guide. What do you have to "Gain"? You have already lost so much. This book allows you to see beyond those storms, clouds, and be at peace and victory. I truly want that for myself. Thank you for your voice Monica, to help us strengthen our voice.

RENEE MCMILLAN

Introduction:
Broken But Not In Pieces
You're Not Alone

There's a kind of pain that doesn't always show on the surface. You can walk into a room with a smile on your face, yet feel like something inside you has cracked. Maybe your heart was broken. Maybe your spirit was **too**. Maybe life hit you so hard, you lost sight of who you were. I wrote this book for you. For the woman who gave everything — and was left with nothing. For the woman who feels like she must keep it all together, even when everything is falling apart. For the woman who is broken but refuses to be in pieces.

Being broken doesn't make you weak. It means you've lived, loved, trusted, and maybe even lost. But you're still here. And you're not alone. This book is a journey — not from broken to perfect, but from broken too whole. We'll walk through pain, healing, rediscovery, and finally, power. You'll hear truths, stories, questions, and maybe even pieces of yourself. Because you're not just broken.

You're rebuilding. And every piece matters.

Notes for Guidance

Losing Myself

"I looked in the mirror and didn't recognize the woman staring back at me. Her eyes were tired, her smile was forced, and her light had dimmed. Somewhere along the way — in loving others, surviving storms, and pretending to be okay — I forgot how to love myself.

Healing Truth

Losing yourself doesn't mean you're lost forever. You can return home to yourself — one honest conversation, one boundary, one act of self-kindness at a time.

Affirmation:

"I may have lost pieces of myself along the way, but I am finding my way back. I am allowed to change, to grow, to come home to the woman I was always meant to be.

Chapter One:
The Breaking Point

"Some people think brokenness happens all at once — like one big explosion. But mine didn't. Mine came quietly, slowly, over time. It came through smiles that hid pain, apologies that meant nothing, and a love that I kept trying to resuscitate long after it had stopped breathing."

Astoundingly married for fifteen years. Fifteen years of memories, ups and downs, promises, and prayers. I wasn't perfect, and neither was he. But I came in with a heart full of love and a willingness to fight for my family. I believed that with enough love, patience, and prayer, anything could be fixed. But by the sixth year, something shifted. It wasn't all bad. That's the hard part — people assume abuse always looks like screaming matches or bruises. Mine came in waves. Long periods of peace, followed by moments of heartbreak. A storm that showed up when I least expected it. Cheating that shattered trust. Words that tore at my soul. The kind of disrespect that doesn't just hurt — it steals pieces of who you are.

And each time, I stayed.

Each time, I forgave.

Each time, I told myself, **maybe this time he'll change.**

I didn't realize how much I was losing. I wore my smile like a mask. I showed up for my family like nothing was wrong. I stayed busy to avoid breaking down. But inside, I was slipping further and further away from the woman I used to be. He took my love for granted.

He thought I would keep accepting the unimaginable — because I had before. And in some ways, he wasn't wrong. I stayed far longer than my heart could handle. I accepted behavior that went against everything I prayed for, all in the name of love and hope. But sometimes, hope hurts when it's placed in the wrong place for too long.

April 2024 was my breaking point.

I didn't throw anything. I didn't scream. I didn't even have the energy to cry. I went cold — not out of hate, but because my soul had nothing left to give. I moved upstairs, and with that, I moved into a place of emotional shutdown. For four months, I said very little. I lived in the same house but in a completely different world. That silence was my survival.

People say silence is passive, but for me, it was strength. I used that time to shut out the noise — the lies, the excuses, the fear — and I turned inward. I turned to God. Not to beg Him to fix my husband. Not to beg Him to fix my marriage. I turned to Him to fix me.

I began fasting. I started praying — deep, raw, tear soaked prayers. I laid everything at His feet. My disappointment. My exhaustion. My confusion. My loneliness. I didn't come to God with pretty words — I came broken, trembling, and real.

And on the third day of my fast, I had a conversation with God that changed everything. "Lord," I said, "if I ever rekindle this marriage, let it be only because You told me to. Not because I feel obligated. Not because I'm afraid to start over. Not because I miss what we had. If I go back into that relationship fully, it will only be because You command it." I meant it.

I told God that I would not accept another round of cheating. No more disrespect. No more abuse. No more chaos. I told Him, *if You restore this, You must make it new* — because I cannot survive another cycle of silent suffering. That prayer wasn't a threat to my husband. It was a declaration of love for me. For the first time in a long time, I chose me. Not in selfishness — but in obedience. Obedience to the God who never wanted me to live in quiet torment. Obedience to the voice that said, *"You are worth more than this."* That moment — that silent, sacred breaking point — was the beginning of my healing. It didn't look dramatic. I didn't pack a bag or slam a door. I just chose peace. And peace sometimes starts with walking away from the war you keep losing yourself in. People ask, "How did you know you were done?" And my answer is this:

I wasn't done loving.

I wasn't done believing in restoration.

But I was done bleeding in places **where I** refused to bandage the wound.

I was done hurting just to keep the image alive. I was done losing myself for the sake of saving someone else's comfort.

That was my breaking point — but not my breakdown.

I didn't fall to pieces. I stood in the middle of my storm, wounded but still standing. I **was** bent, but I didn't break. And that's why this chapter is not about defeat — it's about the moment I stopped trying to survive pain… and started choosing healing.

Reflection: Sometimes, the road to healing doesn't begin with heartbreak — it begins with God quietly calling your name through the voice of someone else. For me, it was a little girl with a heart for heaven and the courage to speak.

PRAYER:

God, thank You for never giving up on me — even when I was running. Thank You for showing up in unexpected places and using unexpected people to call me back to You. Today, I surrender again. Not out of fear. Not out of guilt. But out of love. Amen.

God didn't need me to be perfect — He just needed me to be open. My surrender started the moment I stopped trying to lead my life and let Him take the lead.

Chapter Two:
The Beginning of Surrender

"Sometimes, God doesn't shout. Sometimes He sends a child to whisper His will. And when you're ready to listen, that whisper becomes the roar that changes everything."

It was the last day of the year — **December 31, 2010,** New Year's Eve. I had just left church and was trying to unwind from everything heavy in my life. My cousin and I stopped by a local neighborhood spot. Nothing wild. Just a place to breathe and take the edge off. That night, my life changed — not with fireworks or a dramatic revelation, but with a simple moment.

I met him.

He walked over, introduced himself, smiled, and asked my name. Then he asked if I'd like a drink. We stood there talking casually, nothing serious — until one of his friends walked up, someone he hadn't seen in a while. Without hesitation, the friend looked at us and asked, *"Is that your wife?"*

We both smiled — not knowing that smile would echo through the years ahead, through moments of joy, pain, silence, betrayal, and endurance. At the time, I didn't think much of it. But later, I'd remember that moment as more than just coincidence. It felt like a divine foreshadowing — one I didn't understand yet.

Back then, my life was chaotic.

Outwardly, I functioned. Inwardly, I was unraveling. Emotionally torn. Spiritually split. I knew God was pulling on my heart. I could feel it — that gentle tug that doesn't force you, but refuses to let you go. I was tired. I was numb. I was surviving, not living.

And God was calling me to surrender. But surrender wasn't easy. I didn't want to let go of the life I had grown used to. I didn't understand what true freedom looked like. To me, living "saved" seemed like living stuck. I thought it meant rules, silence, and missing out on fun. I had the wrong perspective — one built on fear and false examples. I didn't yet know that living for God came with peace, joy, identity, and restoration.

I was straddling the fence. One foot in the world, the other hesitant to step into the unknown with God. And like many women, I was good at pretending I was okay — smiling through spiritual exhaustion.

Then came **the night everything shifted**.

I was in my room getting dressed to go out — not just out, but out-out. Puff Daddy was coming to a popular nightclub in town, and that was the plan. Music, lights, fun — everything I thought would give me the escape I needed.

But before I could finish getting ready, my youngest daughter, **Jasmine,** walked in. She looked at me — so small, so serious — and said, "Mama, I want to go to church and get baptized... to go to heaven." I froze for a second. I heard her, but I wasn't really listening. I said, "Okay, Jasmine. I'll take you to church." And then I went right back to doing my makeup, adjusting my outfit, and preparing to walk into a world I no longer fit in.

But God wasn't done yet. She came back — again — and said the same thing, only this time with more urgency in her little voice: *"Mama, I want to go to church and get baptized."* That time, I really heard her. I stopped everything. The music. The outfit. The plans. All of it. And I turned to her with a heart that suddenly felt exposed. I saw something in her eyes — sincerity, hunger, *truth*. And I couldn't ignore it anymore. God had just used my daughter to touch something in me that had been sleeping for years.

That moment marked the beginning.

I took her to church that Sunday. Then again the next Sunday. And again the Sunday after that. It became our new rhythm — not out of duty, but out of desire. Jasmine was consistent. Focused. But what I didn't realize was this: while I was watching her grow spiritually, **God was working on me.**

Little by little, I was changing.

We started going to Sunday school. We joined the greeting team. I started paying attention to the sermons instead of just sitting through them. I found myself singing worship songs during the week. My spirit was waking up. I didn't even recognize the woman I was becoming — and I loved her. She was softer but stronger. More open, less guarded. She was becoming me again. The me, I was, before life hardened me.

One Sunday, Jasmine asked, "Mama, how will I know when it's time?" She meant time to give her life to God. I looked at her, heart full, and said, "When God puts it on your heart, baby, you'll know."

And then it happened. A few Sundays later, Jasmine walked down the aisle **by herself** and gave her life to Jesus. She didn't look back. She didn't wait for me to hold her hand. She knew. And when I saw her standing there at the altar, arms open, heart ready — I broke.

I cried and cried. Not tears of sadness, but of **release.** Something in me gave way. I saw her do what I had been too afraid to do: surrender. And in her surrender, I found mine.

That day, I stopped running. I stopped pretending. I stopped trying to carry it all on my own. I surrendered to God — completely. Not with fear. Not with guilt. But with a heart ready to heal, to rebuild, to rest.

Have you ever had a moment where someone unexpectedly reminded you who you were created to be? Sometimes God doesn't send thunder or fire. Sometimes He sends a child. That moment taught me that God never gave up on me — even when I was halfway in and halfway out. I **went** to church out of routine. Even when I was torn. He waited. Patiently. Lovingly. And He used the very child I thought I was leading... to lead me home.

A PRAYER from My HEART:

A Prayer from My Heart God, thank You for chasing me down with grace. Thank You for loving me even when I didn't love myself enough to walk away from what was breaking me. Thank You for using my daughter to be the light I needed in my darkest place. I surrender again today, with open hands and an open heart. I don't have all the answers, but I trust You, Amen.

I am not disqualified by my past. I am called. I am covered. I am chosen. Even when I was running, God still had a plan for my return. And this time, I'm not turning back.

Notes for Guidance

Chapter Three:
Loving God While Living in Hell

"I was falling in love with God while slowly falling out of love with my husband. My spirit was rising, but my home was falling apart."

After surrendering my heart to God, something in me shifted — permanently. I felt clearer. Lighter. Stronger. The weight I had carried for years began to lift. And for the first time in a long time, I started to see myself again. Not just as a wife, mother, or survivor, but as a woman who had purpose — a woman who deserved peace. But peace didn't come home with me.

While I was growing spiritually, my marriage was sinking emotionally. I had married a man I believed I could build a life with. We had history, memories, and for a long time, I held on to hope. But behind closed doors, I was living in a kind of silent torment — a place where love felt like a weapon and intimacy felt like a trap.

In the beginning, things weren't all bad. There were good times. Moments where I genuinely felt loved and seen. But those moments became fewer and farther apart. And by the sixth year of our marriage, the hurt had started to outweigh the healing. The cheating, the lies, the emotional abuse — it all took its toll. Not just on my heart, but on my sense of worth. He thought I'd never leave. He thought because I loved him, I would keep accepting the unthinkable. And for a while, I did. I kept giving chance after chance. I prayed, cried, forgave, and repeated the cycle until it became normal. But deep down, I was breaking. And God was starting to speak louder than the lies I kept telling myself.

"You don't have to live like this."

"I didn't create you to be mistreated."

"This isn't love. This is bondage."

The more I grew in God, the more out of place I felt in my own home. I would worship in the morning and walk into a war zone by night. I would study the Word and then be called names that crushed my spirit. It felt like I was living in two different worlds — one where I was free, and another where I was a prisoner. But I wasn't ready to walk away. Not yet.

Instead, I went to God — fully. I fasted. I prayed. I cried until my pillow was soaked and my voice was hoarse. In **April of 2024,** I reached my breaking point. It was the last straw. Something in me shut down completely. I went cold. I moved upstairs and emotionally detached.

I wasn't angry.

I was done.

And in that place of silence, I turned to God for direction. I fasted for **three days**, pleading for clarity. I didn't want to make a decision out of anger. I wanted to make a decision out of obedience. On the **third day,** I made a vow to God.

I told Him, "Lord, if I go back, it will only be because You told me to. Not because I'm afraid to be alone. Not because I'm trying to protect a title. If You lead me back, it's only because You have a plan to restore what's been broken." And then I laid it all out.

I told God what I couldn't go through anymore.

No more cheating.

No more lies.

No more disrespect.

No more abuse.

No more walking on eggshells.

No more pretending.

No more begging to be loved.

I told Him that if I were going to stay, it would have to be a marriage rebuilt by His hands, not mine. Because I had nothing left. My love had run dry. My patience had worn thin. My hope had cracked.

"God, if You want me to stay, You have to heal this man, change this home, and protect my heart. Because I'm tired of patching up wounds that never close."

That was one of the most honest prayers I've ever prayed.

Because for once, I wasn't trying to save my marriage — I was trying to save myself. I began to realize something that changed everything: I was not created to endure **pain in place of peace**. I was not born to be someone's emotional punching bag. I am not a doormat. I am not weak for walking away. In fact, it takes more strength to leave a toxic cycle than it does to stay in one. God was not asking me to choose between Him and my marriage. He was asking me to choose between **bondage and freedom.** And I was finally ready to choose freedom.

Faith doesn't exempt you from pain. Sometimes, faith walks you right through the fire — not to burn you, but to purify you.

I had to learn that loving God didn't mean I had to stay in a marriage that was crushing my soul. God doesn't bless chaos. He blesses **obedience.** And when obedience means walking away from what's breaking you — then yes, even that is holy.

PRAYER:

Lord, I love You. And I trust You. But I am tired of hurting in silence. I am tired of waiting on someone to love me right while I keep losing myself. Show me what You want me to do — not what tradition says, not what people say, but what You say. Heal my heart. Heal my mind. And if this chapter is closing, give me the strength to turn the page. Amen.

I am no longer begging to be chosen. I choose myself. I choose peace. I choose healing. And most of all — I choose God's plan over my pain.

Chapter Four:
I Moved Up to Move On

"I didn't leave the house. I just left the war. I moved upstairs — not to escape, but to survive."

April 2024, I'll never forget. After fifteen years of trying to hold it together — the betrayal, the lies, the emotional roller coasters — something in me finally snapped. It wasn't loud. It wasn't dramatic. I didn't scream or break anything. I just went cold.

That was the moment I realized the love I once had for my husband had been slowly bleeding out. Every tear I cried was a drop of love lost. Every time I forgave him for something he never apologized for, I gave up a little more of myself. Until there was nothing left but a woman in pieces — exhausted, empty, and numb. So I moved upstairs. Not out of spite.

Not to punish him. But to find silence. To find God. To find me.

I needed a safe place. And the master bedroom — the place where I once laid my head beside a man who had shattered my heart — no longer felt safe. It felt like a room full of ghosts. Memories of apologies he didn't mean. Nights I cried myself to sleep. Mornings I woke up hoping he'd finally see me — only to be met with distance and disrespect.

So I packed my things, and I went upstairs.

That room became my sanctuary. It became the space where God met me in my brokenness. There were no distractions, no pretending, and no hiding. I laid on that bed and poured out everything I had left. The tears. The rage. The grief of losing a man who was still physically present but emotionally gone.

Upstairs became the place where healing began. I started writing again. I started praying differently.

I started talking to God like He was my best friend — because at that point, He was all I had.

I didn't go to war with my husband.

I went to war **for my soul.**

It wasn't easy. There were days I felt crazy for staying under the same roof. Days I questioned whether God was really listening. Nights when I still heard the echoes of our last argument in my head.

But even in that confusion, there was clarity.

Because for the first time in years — I chose me. I wasn't trying to fix him anymore. I wasn't fighting for us. I wasn't holding on to hope that he would change. I let go of that burden and handed it to God. And I told Him the truth.

"God, I don't even want this anymore unless You change it. Unless You change him, change me, and change this entire atmosphere — I'm done. "And I meant it.

There's a difference between leaving a house and leaving a marriage. I was still present physically. I still made sure the house was running. I still smiled for the kids. But emotionally? Spiritually? I had let go.

Sometimes God doesn't need you to walk out the front door.

Sometimes He needs you to go upstairs — to higher ground.

That upstairs room became my mountain. My place of separation. My place of meeting God face-to face, just like Moses. It was where I received peace in the middle of chaos. Where I began to see that I was more than a wife trying to hold something broken together.

I was a woman becoming whole again.

PRAYER:

Lord, thank You for meeting me in the upstairs room.
Thank You for speaking when
I was too tired to pray out loud.
Thank You for reminding me that separation doesn't
always mean failure — sometimes it's Your protection.
Help me to keep choosing peace, even when it's hard.
Help me not to run back to the things
You've called me away from.
Help me to heal in Your timing, with Your strength.
I moved upstairs not to run, but to rise.
I am not hiding — I am healing.
And every step I take towards wholeness is a step away
from the woman who used to settle.

Chapter Five:
I Lost Me, But I'm Finding Her Again

"I was so busy trying to be everything for him... I forgot who I was for me."

When you spend years surviving instead of living, you eventually forget who you are.

You don't even notice it at first. It happens slowly. Subtly. You start putting your needs last. You quiet your voice to keep the peace. You shrink your dreams so they don't make him uncomfortable. You adjust your light so he doesn't feel overshadowed. And before you know it, the woman you used to be — vibrant, joyful, **lively** — becomes a distant memory. That's what happened to me.

In the beginning, I thought I was just being a good wife. A good woman. I thought love meant sacrificing everything, even myself. I gave and gave and gave — until there was nothing left of me but the roles I played. Wife. Mother. Peacemaker. Provider. Listener. Forgiver.

But, not once did I stop to ask: *What about me?*

What about the woman who used to laugh from her belly?

The woman who danced in the mirror just because she felt beautiful? The woman who had goals, ideas, and dreams long before she said "I do"? She was still there.

Buried. Forgotten. But not gone.

The longer I stayed in a marriage that didn't feed me emotionally or spiritually, the more I faded. And the more I faded, the more he stopped seeing me too. I was existing — but I wasn't *living*. I looked alive on the outside, but inside, I was running on fumes. And then came the silence.

After I moved upstairs and stopped begging to be loved right, I started hearing myself again. For the first time in years, my thoughts weren't drowned out by his voice. My prayers weren't clouded by his chaos. I had room to breathe. Room to grieve. Room to remember who I used to be. That's when the rediscovery began.

The Moment I Knew I Was Gone

One night, I stood in the bathroom looking at my reflection — and I didn't recognize the woman staring back at me. Her eyes were tired. Her shoulders were heavy. Her smile was forced. Her light was dim. And I whispered, "Where did you go?" Tears fell. Because I realized I had been missing for years, and nobody noticed. Not even me. I lost the version of myself that believed she could do anything. I lost the version that refused to settle.

I lost the version that knew her worth.

And the scariest part? I had loved someone else so hard, I didn't leave anything left to love myself.

But God…He stepped in. Quietly. Gently. Constantly.

Every time I cried, He reminded me, *"I still see you."*

Every time I questioned my worth, He whispered, *"You are still mine."* Every time I doubted whether I'd ever feel whole again, He said, *"Daughter, you were never broken beyond repair. You're just buried under years of pain.* But I'm digging you out." I didn't wake up one day completely healed or suddenly confident. No. Rediscovery is a process. And mine was slow, uncomfortable, but beautiful. I started doing small things that brought me joy — things I had stopped doing a long time ago.

- I bought journals and wrote letters to God and to myself.

- I played worship music while cleaning, letting the words wash over my soul.

- I stood in the mirror and complimented myself — even when I didn't feel pretty.

- I took walks and talked to God like He was walking beside me.

- I looked at old pictures — not to feel sad, but to remember the woman I used to be before I let pain change me.

And day by day... she returned.

Stronger. Wiser. Softer, but more secure. Not bitter — just clearer about what she would no longer tolerate.

I started saying "no" without guilt.

I started laughing again — not fake laughter, but real, from-the-gut joy.

I stopped chasing people who didn't value me. And most of all — I started loving myself like I had begged to be loved.

I thought losing him would break me.

But losing myself was the real heartbreak.

It wasn't the abuse that hurt the most — it was the silence I kept to survive it. It wasn't the cheating that destroyed me — it was believing I had to earn loyalty I already deserved.

But I thank God for the process. Because rediscovering myself has been the most powerful journey I've ever walked.

This time, I'm not loving from an empty cup.

This time, I'm not shrinking to be accepted.

This time, I'm not sacrificing my peace for anyone's approval. This time, I know who I am — and I won't lose her again.

When I didn't know I was **still** falling apart, God **helped** me to continue healing, rediscovering, and loving myself as fiercely as **He** love**d** me. I don't want to go back to the version of me that settled for less. I want to walk forward as the woman **He** designed — bold, beautiful, and whole. I am returning to myself. I am not too far gone. God is restoring me — piece by piece, prayer by prayer. The woman I used to be is becoming the woman I was always meant to be.

PRAYER:

Father, thank you for not letting me disappear completely. Thank You for holding the pieces of me together when I didn't even know I was falling apart. Help me to continue healing, rediscovering, and loving myself as fiercely as You love me. I don't want to go back to the version of me that settled for less. I want to walk forward as the woman You designed-Bold, Beautiful, and Whole, In Jesus name. Amen

Notes for Guidance

Chapter Six:
Boundaries Are Holy — Not Harsh

"Even Jesus walked away from people."

For a long time, I thought being a godly woman meant putting up with anything.

I thought I had to be quiet when I was hurt, passive when I was angry, and forgiving no matter how many times someone crossed the same line. I thought that in order to be "submissive," I had to lose my voice. I let people walk over me — and I called it love. I let disrespect slide — and I called it patience. I stayed in places where I was slowly dying — and I called it faith.

But God had to teach me something I didn't hear in church growing up:

Boundaries are not rebellion. Boundaries are not bitterness. Boundaries are biblical.

The Wake-Up Call

One day, during my time alone with God, I was reading through the book of Proverbs. I wasn't looking for anything deep — I just wanted wisdom. But when I got to Proverbs 4:23, it stopped me:

> *"Above all else, guard your heart, for everything you do flows from it."*
>
> — PROVERBS 4:23 (NIV)

I had read that verse a hundred times. But that day, it hit differently.

It didn't say, *"Let everyone have unlimited access to your heart."*

It said, "Guard it."

Not everyone deserves a front-row seat in your life.

Not everyone deserves constant access to your emotions.

Not everyone deserves to pull from you without ever pouring back into you.

That verse gave me **permission** — no, **instruction** — to protect what God was building in me. I had spent years leaving the doors of my heart wide open, and people came in and trashed the place. Now I understood why I felt so drained, so broken, so lost.

I wasn't guarding my heart.

I was exposing it to damage — over and over again.

Boundaries With My Husband

The first person I had to set boundaries with was my husband. And that was one of the hardest things I ever had to do.

It started with one simple boundary: *"You cannot speak to me any kind of way anymore and still expect intimacy, respect, or peace."*

I didn't scream. I didn't deliver it with an attitude. I said it calmly, but firmly — and with God's authority behind me.

He didn't like it.

But that didn't matter anymore.

God reminded me:

> *"Fear of man will prove to be a snare, but whoever trusts in the Lord is kept safe."*
>
> — Proverbs 29:25 (NIV)

For too long, I had feared what he would do if I spoke up. Would he leave? Would he stop providing? Would he get angrier?

But the real question was: **What would I lose if I kept being silent?**

I was losing my peace.

I was losing my identity.

I was losing my connection with God — trying to maintain a connection with someone who didn't even value me.

I started to draw lines.

- I stopped arguing to be understood.
- I stopped letting guilt manipulate me into saying "yes" when my spirit was screaming "no."
- I stopped lowering my standards for the sake of "keeping the peace" — because it wasn't peace. It was quiet chaos.
- I gave myself permission to say no — and mean it.

It wasn't just him. I had to set boundaries with family members, friends, and even church folks.

Some people only loved the broken version of me — the one who said "yes" to everything and never pushed back. But once I started healing and setting limits, they called me "changed." They said I was "acting differently."

They were right.

I had changed. And I wasn't going back.

I learned that setting boundaries is **not about being mean**. It's about being healthy.

Even Jesus had boundaries.

He walked away from crowds (Luke 5:16).

He said "no" to people's demands (John 6:15).

He didn't allow everyone into His inner circle (Matthew 17:1).

He even flipped tables in the temple when people disrespected His Father's house (Matthew 21:12–13).

So if Jesus could walk away, if Jesus could set standards, if Jesus could say "enough" — then so can I.

> *"Do not be misled: 'Bad company corrupts good character.'"*
>
> — 1 Corinthians 15:33 (NIV)

If God is trying to make me whole, I can't stay surrounded by people — even loved ones — who are pulling me back into brokenness.

I used to think being godly meant being a doormat.

Now I know better.

God didn't call me to be walked on — He called me to walk boldly.

God didn't ask me to suffer in silence — He asked me to speak truth in love.

God didn't tell me to stay In toxic places — He told me to guard my heart.

And now, I choose peace over performance.

I choose boundaries over burnout.

I choose wholeness over toxic loyalty.

PRAYER:

Lord, help me to protect what You are building in me. Give me the courage to say "no" without guilt and me the wisdom to draw lines where You need me to. I don't have to explain my boundaries to people who benefitted from me having none. I protect my peace because I finally know my worth. God is not asking me to be passive — He's asking me to be wise. Boundaries are not walls to keep people out — they are gates to protect what matters inside.

Notes for Guidance

Chapter Seven:
When He Walked Out, God Walked In

*"Sometimes, God has to remove what we think we need
— so we can see He was all we ever truly needed."*

I will never forget that day.

It was the third day of my fast. I had been crying out to God, asking Him for clarity, for direction, for peace — and most of all, for a sign. I laid everything before Him. I told Him I couldn't take the pain anymore — the cheating, the abuse, the constant disrespect, the confusion. I told Him I was done living a lie, pretending everything was fine when I was falling apart inside.

I said:

"God, if I'm going to fight for this marriage, let it be because You told me to — not because I'm afraid of being alone."

I told Him what I couldn't accept anymore.

I gave Him every tear, every fear, every ounce of heartbreak I had carried silently for years. And on that third day… **my husband walked out.**

When the Provider Left

I stood in the house, stunned.

I had just surrendered everything to God — and now, the man who had shared my life for 15 years was gone. It felt like the air had been sucked out of the room. I stared at the door for what felt like forever, half-expecting him to walk back through it. But he didn't. And fear hit me hard.

How would I pay these bills?

How would I take care of the house?

How would I survive?

For so long, I believed *he* was the provider.

He brought stability.

He helped keep everything going. It wasn't that he was perfect — far from it — but I had grown used to depending on him, even though the chaos.

But in that quiet moment, when I could no longer deny that he was truly gone, God whispered something to my spirit I'll never forget:

"He was never your provider. I was. I always have been."

✝ **Philippians 4:19** says,

"And my God will meet all your needs according to the riches of his glory in Christ Jesus."

I had trusted a man to carry what only God could sustain.

In that moment, I felt a shift. My fear began to turn into something else — a strange mix of peace and conviction. It was as if God was inviting me to stop placing my security in people, and to start seeing Him as the source.

The very next month, when bills came due — God moved.

I didn't know how I was going to manage all the bills — at the restaurant and at home — at the same time.

I remember sitting at the kitchen table, staring at the numbers — looking at the bills, sales expenses, payroll & inventory — and my chest felt tight. There were no easy answers.

But I kept praying.

I kept trusting. I kept saying,

"God, I told you I'd trust You. I meant that. I don't know what's coming next, but I know you're in it."

Then, out of nowhere — a door opened.

A catering opportunity came my way from someone I knew. I wasn't out searching for it. It just showed up, like a whisper straight from heaven.

When I saw the amount it paid, I stopped in my tracks.

It was the exact amount my husband used to help cover the bills.

That wasn't a coincidence. That was confirmation.

God was saying, *"I've got you — and I've got this."*

✝ Psalm 37:25 says,

"I have been young, and now am old; yet have I not seen the righteous forsaken, nor his seed begging bread."

He didn't just give me money.

He gave me **evidence** that I was **never alone**.

He gave me proof that **He provides when people walk away.**

He gave me confidence to know — I wasn't just surviving this. I was being carried through it by His hand.

✝ **Deuteronomy** 31:6 says,

"Be strong and courageous. Do not be afraid or terrified because of them, for the Lord your God goes with you; He will never leave you nor forsake you."

That day, I made a vow and gain a New Covenant With God

"Lord, I will walk through this process — faithful to You. I will not look back. I will not chase after what You've allowed to walk away. I will trust You with everything in me. My finances. My healing. My future. My wholeness. My joy. My identity. All of it. I'm Yours."

I made up my mind: no matter how long this healing journey took, I would walk it out **hand-in-hand with God.**

And that changed everything.

I started to see God in the little things — unexpected favors, doors opening, peace that didn't make sense. He wasn't just my Provider… He became my **Companion**, my **Comforter**, my **Counselor**, and the **Lover of my soul**.

✝ **Isaiah 41:10** says,

"So do not fear, for I am with you; do not be dismayed, for I am your God. I will strengthen you and help you; I will uphold you with my righteous right hand."

I started journaling my prayers. I kept a list of the ways God showed up — big and small. Every time He answered a prayer, even if it was just a moment of peace or a stranger's kindness, I wrote it down. These reminders became my survival kit. My journal wasn't just a place to vent — it became my testimony in progress.

I won't lie and say I wasn't still scared sometimes. I was. There were nights I cried myself to sleep. Days I didn't know how I'd get out of bed. Moments when loneliness screamed louder than my prayers.

But each time fear crept in, I'd go back to what God had already done. I'd remind myself: *He provided last time — He'll do it again.*

He carried me before — He's not about to drop me now.

2 Timothy 1:7 says,

"For God hath not given us the spirit of fear; but of power, and of love, and of a sound mind."

I learned that faith isn't the absence of fear — it's the decision to trust God even when fear shows up.

And that trust gave me power.

I no longer had to beg a man to stay.

I no longer had to fear walking alone.

I no longer had to compromise my soul to keep a roof over my head.

I had a **Heavenly Father** who was showing up, stepping in, and pouring out more than I even asked for.

Ephesians 3:20 says,

"Now unto him that is able to do exceeding abundantly above all that we ask or think, according to the power that worketh in us."

I used to think my husband walking out would be the worst thing that could ever happen to me.

But it turned out to be the **doorway to my deliverance.**

Because when he walked out — **God walked in deeper.**

And God didn't come to rescue me temporarily — He came to **rebuild me permanently.**

I don't cry over what left anymore.

Because what left made room for what I needed most:

My Father's love, provision, and presence.

Romans 8:28 says,

"And we know that all things work together for good to them that love God, to them who are the called according to his purpose."

God is my provider not people. God is my protector, not circumstances. God is my strength, not fear when people walk out. God shows up, and he never leaves me.

"Weeping may endure for a night, but joy comes in the morning."
— PSALM 30:5

But rest didn't come easy.

The Sleepless Nights

I had so many sleepless nights. Some nights my spiritual mother would talk with me on the phone until 3 a.m., or until I could finally fall asleep. The night was always the hardest time — because now I was coming home to an empty house. The silence felt louder than any argument we ever had. I was so broken that I didn't even recognize the emotions I was feeling — I was experiencing grief for the first time in years.

It was easy to keep a straight face during the day. I had mastered the art of smiling through pain. I walked with my head held high and a smile on my face, but deep inside I was carrying shame and hurt. I had already learned how to walk in shame during my marriage — when he cheated on me, when he dated women in my face, and when everyone around us knew what was happening. That shame was heavy.

But the shame of a broken marriage? That hit differently. I was hurting so badly that I forgot something powerful: God had answered my prayer. God had given my husband the strength — or the release — to walk away because He didn't want me to keep hurting anymore. I asked for God's direction. I asked for freedom from the pain. And in His mercy... He delivered it. Even in my brokenness, God was being faithful. Even when I forgot what I prayed for, God didn't forget His promise. Letting go wasn't just about releasing my husband — it was about releasing the image I had created in my mind. I had built a fantasy around what I thought marriage should be. I clung to potential instead of reality. But God was calling me into truth.

John 8:32 says, "Then you will know the truth,
and the truth will set you free."
And the truth was — I deserved more.
More peace. More respect. More love. More honesty. More of God.
But to receive more, I had to let go of less. I had to trust that even though I didn't understand everything, God wasn't confused. He knew what He was doing. And in the letting go, I was learning how to live open-handed.
"Let go of what you thought it had to be — so God can show you what it's meant to be."
Everyday I woke up and chose faith — even when I didn't feel it. I chose to read Scripture. I chose to journal. I chose to pray. And over time, I noticed something: my faith was growing muscles. The things that used to crush me didn't hit the same anymore. The opinions of others started to fade into the background. I was building spiritual stamina.
Hebrews 11:1 says, *"Now faith is the substance of things hoped for, the evidence of things not seen."*
I couldn't see what was next — but I believed something better was coming.
Romans 10:17 says, *"So then faith comes by hearing, and hearing by the word of God."*
So I stayed close to the Word. I surrounded myself with worship.

I listened to sermons, played gospel music in my house, and filled my atmosphere with truth.

And my atmosphere started changing.

A Legacy of Broken Silence

"Submit to one another out of reverence for Christ."

— Ephesians 5:21

As I reflect on the brokenness I experienced in my marriage, I can't help but think about my grandmother. I think about the generations of women who came before me — women who endured, sacrificed, and stayed silent through unbearable hurt. They were strong in ways the world never gave them credit for. They bore their pain quietly, in the name of loyalty and in the name of marriage.

My grandmother, like so many others, was taught that to be a good wife meant to suffer in silence. She stayed faithful through disrespect, overlooked betrayal, and kept her household together — even when her own heart was falling apart. She wasn't weak. She was committed. But that kind of commitment came with a cost. I watched the pattern repeat in my own life.

When my marriage began to fall apart, I carried that same mindset. I told myself to hold on. I reminded myself of the vows I took. I believed that if I just prayed more, served more, forgave more — things would get better. And for a long time, I confused endurance with righteousness.

Yes, the Bible tells wives to submit to their husbands. But the part that rarely gets spoken aloud in the church is this:

"Husbands, love your wives, just as Christ loved the church and gave himself up for her." — Ephesians 5:25

Submission is mutual. Marriage is not a hierarchy — it's a partnership. God designed marriage to reflect His covenant with us: one of love, sacrifice, respect, and unity.

What I experienced was far from that.

The longer I stayed silent about the cheating, the disrespect, and the emotional neglect, the more I lost pieces of myself. I told myself that covering his sin was protecting our marriage. But the truth is — I was enabling it. I was slowly dying emotionally, spiritually, and mentally.

Marriage is hard. But it's not meant to be harmful. A healthy marriage takes two people willing to do the work. Two people submitted to God. Two people ready to forgive, communicate, and rebuild — together.

> *"Can two walk together,* **except** *they be agreed?"*
> — Amos 3:3

When one person is carrying the entire burden, it's no longer a union — it's a slow death.

One thing marriage taught me is that forgiveness is necessary — not just once, but over and over again. Forgiveness is essential to healing. But forgiveness without truth is dangerous. I had to learn to tell myself the truth: that my marriage wasn't honoring God or myself.

Forgiveness doesn't always mean reconciliation. Sometimes it means release. I had to forgive him for the pain he caused. But I also had to forgive myself — for staying silent for so long, for shrinking myself to keep peace, for believing I had to suffer to be a good wife.

> *"And you will know the truth, and the truth will set you free."*
> — John 8:32

Freedom came the moment I stopped pretending. Despite everything I went through, I still believe in marriage. I believe in love. I believe in restoration. But I believe it must be built on truth.

Marriage can be one of the most beautiful unions on earth — when both people invite God in. It takes humility. It takes work. It takes daily surrender.

I've come to understand that God never asked me to abandon myself for the sake of a title. He asked me to trust Him. He asked me to be obedient, to speak the truth in love, and to choose healing over hiding.

So I broke the silence. I broke the pattern. And in that breaking, I found myself.

"He heals the brokenhearted and binds up their wounds."

— PSALM 147:3

Notes for Guidance

PRAYER:

Father, thank You for being faithful. Thank You for showing me that even when people leave, You stay. You provide. You carry. You lead. I trust You now with everything — even the parts that scare me. Keep showing me that I don't have to beg for what You are willing to give freely. I trust You with my heart, my healing, and my hope. In Jesus' name, Amen

Chapter Eight:
Faith in the Fire

*"When you pass through the waters, I will be with you; and
through the rivers, they shall not overflow you. When you
walk through the fire, you shall not be burned, nor shall the
flame scorch you."*

— Isaiah 43:2

Walking with God doesn't mean you won't feel the heat — it just means you won't be consumed by it. After my husband walked out, the days that followed felt like I was standing in fire. Everything around me was unfamiliar. My routines changed. My thoughts were loud. My heart was raw. I was walking into a brand-new life, but I had no road map. The only thing I had left to hold on to, was **my** faith.

And truthfully? That faith was shaky.

There is a different kind of fire that comes when the old has left but the new hasn't fully arrived. I was in that place. Emotionally, spiritually, and even physically, I felt like I was in the middle of a breakdown. But the more I pressed into prayer, the more I began to realize — it wasn't a breakdown… it was a **refining.**

1 Peter 1:6–7 says, "In this you greatly rejoice, though now for a little while you may have had to suffer grief in all kinds of trials. These have come so that the proven genuineness of your faith — of greater worth than gold, which perishes even though refined by fire — may result in praise, glory and honor when Jesus Christ is revealed." God wasn't punishing me — He was purifying me. Every tear I cried was cleansing my spirit. Every quiet night alone was an invitation to sit with God. Every unanswered question was pushing me to open His Word and find new answers. My fear didn't disqualify my faith — it deepened it. Because every time I feared what was coming next, I'd hear that still, small voice remind me:

"You're not alone. I'm in the fire with you." Think about the three Hebrew boys in *Daniel 3:23-25*. This has always been one of my favorite scriptures because, in life, we all go through trials and tribulations. The pain of our circumstances can make us feel like we are alone. But the truth is, God is always standing right there with us in the middle of it all.

The three Hebrew boys were confident that God would deliver them no matter what. Their faith was tested when King Nebuchadnezzar threw them into the fiery furnace, yet in the fire, the king realized something amazing-there was a fourth man with them.

How many times have we gone through trials and felt completely alone? That's how the enemy plays on our emotions and preys on our feelings. But the reality is, when we put our trust in God, we are never alone in any fire or furance. Even if we can't see Him with our natural eyes, He is there with us in a spiritual way. *So, I say this to you: it is good to go through when Jesus is on your side-because no matter how hot the fire is, you will not be consumed. You will come out stronger, refined, and victorious, because the Son of God is standing with you.*

Now, as your mind drifts back to those memories when you were in the fire, remember how God's healing hand carried you through. It was your faith that allowed you to walk out with His grace, stronger than when you went in.

But today, I want to speak to the person who is still under the fire. Maybe you've faced the pain of a divorce, the ache of separation, or the loss of a spouse. In moments like these, the temptation to rush ahead is strong-but hear me: ***healing takes time.*** Moving too quickly can send you right back into an uncertain situation, and brokenness that is left unchecked can shatter into pieces.

This is your season to pause. Take time to rediscover who you are. Take time to readjust your life, even if it means stepping away from the familiar. And most importantly, take this time to redefine your relationship with God. Every moment you dedicate to Him, He will meet you there-providing clarity, direction, and wisdom to make sound decisions.

Don't be too hasty to step into another relationship when the wounds from the last one haven't fully healed. True healing begins when you surrender your heart completely to God and allow Him to make you whole again. Only then will you be prepared to walk into your next season with peace, strength, and purpose.

PRAYER:

Faith isn't about having all the answers — it's about trusting the One who does. I didn't have it all together. I didn't always feel strong. But I kept showing up. I kept choosing God. I kept walking — even when I couldn't see the road. Because that's what faith is. "Faith doesn't always take the pain away — but it does give the pain a purpose."I am walking by faith, not fear. I am not alone — God is with me in the fire. I am being refined, not destroyed. Something greater is on the other side of this.

Notes for Guidance

Chapter Nine:
Learning to Trust Again

"Trust in the Lord with all your heart and lean not on your own understanding; in all your ways submit to Him, and He will make your paths straight."

— Proverbs 3:5–6

Trust. That word used to feel so heavy. After everything I had been through — the betrayal, the lies, the broken promises — trusting again felt like climbing a mountain barefoot. My heart was raw. My mind was guarded. And every time someone tried to get close, my soul would flinch. But healing requires risk. And trusting again was part of the healing process **that** I could no longer avoid.

When trust is broken, it doesn't just damage your relationship with the other person — it damages your relationship with yourself. I started questioning my own judgment. How did I not see the signs? How did I stay so long? How did I let it get this far? And then came the guilt. The shame. The silence.

"The Lord is near to the brokenhearted and saves the crushed in spirit."

— PSALM 34:18

God didn't shame me — He stayed with me. Through the nights of doubt and the days of confusion, He gently reminded me that He was still trustworthy. That even if people fail, He never would. Before I could trust anyone else, I had to reestablish trust with God. And that meant surrendering the need to understand everything. That meant releasing control, letting go of the "why," and trusting Him with the "what now."

I started praying differently. Not just for answers, but for peace. Not just for direction, but for surrender.

"You will keep in perfect peace those whose minds are steadfast, because they trust in you."

— ISAIAH 26:3

When I placed my pain in His hands, He placed His strength in my heart. One of the hardest people to trust after trauma is yourself. I had to learn to trust my instincts again. To trust the voice of the Holy Spirit within me. To stop second-guessing what I knew to be true.

God began to remind me that discernment is a gift — and it had always been inside me. I just needed to stop silencing it to please others.

Healing meant listening to myself. Honoring my boundaries. Believing that I was worth protecting. *"She is clothed with strength and dignity; she can laugh at the days to come."* — Proverbs 31:25

Trusting again doesn't mean letting everyone in. It means being wise, being prayerful, and being open to God's timing. It means believing that not everyone is sent to hurt you. Some people are sent to help you heal.

I started to see love in small places again: in friendships, in safe conversations, in gentle encouragement from others. It reminded me that trust isn't just about romance — it's about relationship.

> *"Two are better than one, because they have a good return for their labor: If either of them falls down, one can help the other up."*
>
> — *ECCLESIASTES* 4:9–10

God was slowly surrounding me with people who didn't want to take from me — but pour into me.

The Battle Within

So many times I wanted to allow my husband to come back and start over, but I didn't know how to trust him or how to start trusting him. There was a constant battle in my heart between longing for restoration and guarding myself from more pain. As time passed, I realized that a broken marriage is like grief — feelings would come out of nowhere, and I'd find myself asking, "Is there a possibility this marriage can recover? Can we move through the hurt and heal?"

Some days, hope would whisper, "Maybe things could be different this time." Other days, fear would scream, "Don't be a fool. You remember the nights you cried, the silence, the betrayal." The push and pull wore me down. I found myself staring at the door of opportunity — one side labeled "forgiveness," the other "protection." I didn't want to live in bitterness, but I also didn't want to live in denial.

There were moments I'd think back to the man I once fell in love with, wondering if any piece of him still existed. Was it possible to trust someone who had broken the very foundation of our covenant? Could I unlearn the defense mechanisms I had built just to survive the pain?

I began to realize that trusting again didn't start with him — it had to start with God. My faith had to become bigger than my fear. Healing had to become more important than holding onto control. I had to surrender the outcome and let God deal with his heart, while He dealt with mine.

I cried out to God often — not always with words, but with tears that carried more weight than any sentence I could form. I asked Him, "Lord, how do I trust someone who gave me every reason not to? How do I keep my heart open when I feel so exposed?"

And God would gently remind me that trust doesn't mean rushing ahead — it means taking steps, slowly, intentionally, with Him in the lead. I wasn't asked to pretend like nothing happened, but I was called to be honest, to heal, and to choose whether I would walk in faith or stay trapped in fear.

The real battle wasn't just with my husband — it was within me. I was wrestling with disappointment, unmet expectations, and the shattered pieces of a future I once dreamed of. I had to come to terms with the fact that even if we never made it back to each other, I could still heal. I could still forgive. I could still be whole.

Trust is not a one-time decision. It's a daily surrender. It's choosing to believe again — not blindly, but bravely. And as hard as it was, I learned that healing doesn't always mean returning to what broke you. Sometimes healing is allowing God to rebuild you — piece by piece — with or without the person you once prayed for.

PRAYER:

*A Prayer I SAID EVERYDAY. Lord, I'm ready to trust again —
starting with You. Help me to heal the broken pieces within me.
Show me how to trust myself, others, and the process of healing.
Lead me with wisdom, surround me with truth, and fill me with
peace. In Jesus' name, Amen.*

Notes for Guidance

Chapter Ten:
When Restoration Begins in You

"And the God of all grace, who called you to His eternal glory in Christ, after you have suffered a little while, will Himself restore you and make you strong, firm and steadfast."

— 1 PETER 5:10

Restoration doesn't always begin with reconciliation; — it begins with healing. It begins with surrender. It begins with a decision to stop bleeding in silence and start healing out loud. Restoration meant my husband would come back, say all the right things, and we would somehow pick up where we left off. But I've learned that true restoration starts on the inside — and sometimes, it's a journey you walk with God alone before anyone else joins the path.

Before I could ask God to restore my marriage, I had to ask Him to restore me.

There were pieces of me buried under years of pretending. Parts of me lost to silence, shame, fear, and exhaustion. I needed to reclaim my identity — not as a wife, not even as a mother — but as a daughter of the King.

I needed to be reminded that my value wasn't based on who stayed or who left. It was rooted in the One who never changes.

"Fear not, for I have redeemed you; I have called you by name, you are mine."
— Isaiah 43:1

God wanted to restore the woman inside of me before He could ever restore the title of wife. And when I began to heal, to grow, to rise — I started to realize that my healing wasn't just for me. It was for every woman who came after me.

There were days I still longed for the marriage I dreamed of. I wanted to hear the words, "I'm sorry," and "Let's start over." I hoped for a day when we could hold hands and rebuild what had been broken.

But I also knew I couldn't go back to what broke me.

Marriage is a covenant, but it only works when both people are committed to it. I had spent years carrying it alone. And though I was still praying for my husband, I finally realized that I could not force transformation. Only God could do that.

"Unless the Lord builds the house, the builders labor in vain."
— Psalm 127:1

If our marriage was going to be rebuilt, God had to be the foundation. Letting go wasn't giving up — it was giving it to God. I had to release control. I had to release the outcome. I had to stop checking for change and instead focus on my own.

And something happened when I did: I found peace.

I stopped waiting to be chosen and started choosing myself. I stopped obsessing over "what if" and started thanking God for "what is." I realized that healing wasn't just a destination — it was a daily walk. One moment of surrender at a time. One whispered prayer at a time. One act of obedience at a time.

> *"He restores my soul. He leads me in paths of righteousness for His name's sake."*
>
> — Psalm 23:3

If restoration includes reconciliation, it will only be because it's God-ordained and Holy Spirit-led. I still believe in marriage. I still believe God can change hearts. But I also believe restoration begins when I stop waiting to be rescued and start walking in redemption.

Should my husband return — it would have to be a new man who returned to a new woman. One who had met God in the dark and learned to dance in the light.

> *"Behold, I am doing a new thing; now it springs forth, do you not perceive it?"*
>
> — Isaiah 43:19

I gave every broken piece to God. He Restore me from the inside out. Heal every scar, mend every wound, and prepare my heart for whatever want was next. I am being restored from the inside out.

I trust God's plan, even when I don't see it. I release the pain of my past to make room for my future.

My healing is not dependent on others — it begins in me.

PRAYER:

Father, I thank You for starting the work of restoration within me. What was broken, You are making whole; what was lost, You are redeeming. I surrender every piece of my life to Your hands, trusting that Your healing will finish what it began. May my story be a light for others to believe that true restoration always starts with You. Amen

Chapter Eleven:
Finding New Strength in the Aftermath

"But those who hope in the Lord will renew their strength. They will soar on wings like eagles; they will run and not grow weary, they will walk and not be faint."

— Isaiah 40:31

After the dust settles, after the final tear dries, after the silence becomes your new normal — there is a sacred moment where you realize: *I made it.*

You don't always recognize strength in the middle of the storm. But once it passes, you look back and see the evidence. You see the prayers that held you. The peace that surprised you. The strength that was built day by day, silently and steadily.

That's where I found myself — not fully healed, not completely whole, but stronger than I had ever been.

There were nights I didn't think I'd survive the weight of lone-liness. There were mornings I had to remind myself to breathe. But somewhere between the heartbreak and the healing, God was doing something in me.

He was strengthening me.

> *"My grace is sufficient for you, for My power is made perfect in weakness."*
>
> — 2 CORINTHIANS 12:9.

I stopped measuring strength by how much I could endure and started recognizing it in how much I could release. I learned that strength wasn't pretending to be okay — it was choosing to rise even when I wasn't.

Without the weight of trying to fix a broken marriage, I began rediscovering who I was. Not the woman shaped by pain — but the woman molded by purpose.

I started doing things I had set aside for years. I poured into my daughters. I picked up my journal. I started praying for myself, not just others. I began to dream again — and not just about survival, but about joy.

> *"For I know the plans I have for you,"* declares the Lord, *"plans to prosper you and not to harm you, plans to give you hope and a future."*
>
> — JEREMIAH 29:11

God had a plan for me — and it wasn't tied to staying broken.

Joy After Mourning

One morning, I looked in the mirror and realized something had shifted. I didn't cry brushing my teeth. I didn't dread the quiet anymore. I saw peace where pain once lived.

It wasn't sudden. It didn't come all at once. But joy started showing up again — in worship, in walks, in small laughs that didn't feel forced. I wasn't just surviving. I was starting to live again.

Then, I start walking in Strength. I learned it isn't loud. It's not always bold or visible. Sometimes strength is silent. It's in the choice to try again. To open your heart. To forgive. To rebuild. To believe. Walking in strength means I don't wait until everything is perfect to praise God. I praise Him *as* He perfects me. And in every step forward, I remind myself:

I am not what I lost. I am who God is building.

One of the Hardest Storms: When Brokenness Goes Public

One of the hardest things in life is going through a storm — publicly.

My husband and I were what some would call a "power couple." We were building a life together, raising our children, encouraging others, and pouring into our community. People admired our strength, our teamwork, and our story. What they didn't know was that behind the smiles and matching outfits, there was a slow unraveling taking place — one that only I could feel every day. When the lights are on and the crowd that once cheered now sits in silence — some even whispering in the shadows about the weight you carry — that pain hits differently.

Hence, it's one thing to **suffer** in private. **However,** it's **much worse** when your brokenness becomes everybody's business.

Public Eyes, Private Pain

When things started falling apart in my marriage, I didn't just grieve in silence — I grieved under a spotlight.

People noticed when I stopped showing up to events with him. They whispered when I smiled less or kept my head down. They speculated about where he was and what was happening — not realizing that I was still trying to process it myself. I cried in parking lots. I answered text messages with fake emojis. I worshiped in church with a broken heart and greeted people while silently screaming inside. It was like living a double life: strong on the outside, shattered on the inside. I wasn't just losing a marriage. I was losing the image, the comfort, and the community that came with it.

The Silence behind the Smile

The silence hurt the most.

I didn't always feel like I had a safe space to speak. I didn't want to seen as weak. I didn't want pity. I didn't want judgment. And I definitely didn't want to be the center of gossip. So I smiled. I served. I kept going.

But inside, I felt like I was fading. In that stillness, I began to understand that even when people don't understand your pain, God does. And even when no one stands by your side, He stands with you. When the noise around me got loud, I had to go deeper in God. I started waking up early just to cry in His presence. I stopped asking people for answers and started asking Him for peace. And slowly, God started rebuilding me.

He showed me that identity isn't rooted in public approval — it's rooted in His truth. He reminded me that even if people misunderstood, rejected, or judged me — He still called me chosen, loved, and His.

"You are altogether beautiful, my darling;
there is no flaw in you."

— SONG OF SOLOMON 4:7

Public storms will test you in ways private ones never could. They will force you to decide: Will I perform, or will I heal?

I chose to heal. I let go of pretending. I gave myself permission to feel. And I started trusting God to vindicate me, to cover me, and to restore me — not just in public, but in the quiet places of my soul.

If you're in a season where your pain is visible and your healing feels slow, know this: **God sees you.** He is not embarrassed by your brokenness. He is not surprised by your struggle. And He's not done writing your story.

You will rise again — and when you do, you'll walk in a strength no spotlight can give and no storm can take away.

My pain may be public, but so will my healing. God is rewriting my story, not ending it. I am not who they say I am — I am who God says I am. I will heal, grow, and rise again.

PRAYER:

Lord, thank You for meeting me in the ruins and breathing life into what felt lost. In the aftermath, You have been my anchor, my healer, and my strength. I walk forward not in my own power, but in Yours, knowing that every ending with You is the beginning of something greater. Amen

Chapter Twelve:
Rising From the Ashes

"He gives beauty for ashes, the oil of joy for mourning, the garment of praise for the spirit of heaviness..."

— Isaiah 61:3

There comes a point when you have cried your last tear for a person who chose not to fight for you. There comes a moment when you stop looking back at what could have been — and start walking forward into what *will be*.

That moment, for me, was quiet. It didn't come with loud applause or a grand revelation. It came in the stillness — when I finally chose *me*.

For so long, I carried shame for a marriage that failed. I felt like I had disappointed everyone — my children, my church, my friends, and most of all, God. I didn't realize I was still carrying the pressure to make something work that was already broken beyond repair. But healing showed me something: **I wasn't called to fix him — I was called to free me.** I had done everything I knew to do. I prayed. I had fasted. I had forgiven more times than I could count. And yet, nothing has changed. Or rather — *he* didn't change. But *I* did.

And that was the beginning of my rise.

The Breaking Was Also the Becoming

What felt like the end was actually **a new** beginning.

The breaking of my marriage was the birthing of my purpose. God used the ashes of my pain to reveal the gold of my calling. I started writing again. I began to speak to women who had been through the same silent suffering. I looked in the mirror and saw a woman who had walked through fire — and didn't smell like smoke. I was no longer the same woman who begged to be seen, loved, or chosen.

I was the woman who had chosen herself. I was the woman God had chosen all along.

> *"Before I formed you in the womb I knew you,*
> *before you were born I set you apart..."*
> — JEREMIAH 1:5

Every scar told a story. Every tear became a seed. And every "no" I heard in that marriage created space for a divine "yes" from God.

Reclaiming My Voice, My Joy, My Identity

I began to feel joy again — not just fake laughter, but *real* joy. I started loving my life again. I saw my daughters watching me, not just survive — but **thrive**. I stopped shrinking to make others comfortable. I stopped explaining my healing. I stopped apologizing for setting standards.

God was giving me beauty for ashes. He was restoring *me* — not as a wife, but as a *woman of God*.

No longer bound by shame. No longer defined by what was broken. No longer chained to someone else's choices.

I was free.

And freedom look**ed** good on me.

PRAYER:

Father, thank You for never leaving me — even when I felt lost. Thank You for turning my pain into purpose, my mourning into dancing, and my brokenness into beauty. Help me to continue walking in the freedom You've given me. Help me to never go back to what You delivered me from. In Jesus' name, Amen

I am rising from the ashes. I am walking in my purpose. I am healed, whole, and held by God. This is not the end — it's my new beginning.

Chapter Thirteen:
Guarding Grace — What Family Saw and What They Didn't

"A time to be silent and a time to speak..."
— ECCLESIASTES 3:7

One of the hardest parts of going through a broken marriage isn't just what you experience — it's what your family sees. When the people closest to you begin to notice the change in your energy, your joy, and your behavior, they start to put the pieces together. Some of them knew long before you ever said a word. Some suspected but waited for you to speak. And some were blindsided — and hurt because they weren't prepared to see you hurting.

But as I walked through my healing, I learned this:
You don't owe everyone every detail.

The Power of Private Pain

I spent so much time trying to keep things together that I forgot how visible my pain had become.

The way I moved. The way I stopped laughing. The way I kept to myself more. My family saw it, even when I tried to cover it up with makeup, fake smiles, and polite "I'm fine" answers.

What they saw was a woman surviving. What they didn't always know was what I was surviving *through*.

> *"Do not let your left hand know what your right hand is doing."*
> — MATTHEW 6:3

There's wisdom in discretion. Even when things fall apart publicly, you get to decide what part of your story others get to hold. Not because you're hiding — but because you're healing.

Being Mindful of What You Share

It was tempting to vent everything. To talk about the betrayal, the cheating, the lies, and the manipulation. To name names and give details. But I had to ask myself: **What would it fix?**

Would it bring peace or add more fuel to the pain? Would it free me or trap me in the cycle of rehearsing the hurt?

I chose my words carefully. I spoke truth — but I didn't speak from bitterness. I protected my healing by not giving people more ammunition than wisdom. And honestly, I did it for *me*, not him.

> *"Set a guard over my mouth, Lord;*
> *keep watch over the door of my lips."*
> — PSALM 141:3

Family Needs Grace Too

It's easy to forget that your family is grieving too — even if they didn't live inside the marriage.

They may feel helpless, angry, or even guilty for not stepping in. Some may take your pain personally. Some may lash out at your ex or overstep boundaries trying to protect you. But I had to remind myself: **they love me — they just don't always know how to show it.**

So I extended grace. I gently redirected conversations. I gave updates without giving away my peace. I honored the fact that some things were between me and God alone.

Strength Is in the Silence

There's strength in knowing when to speak and when to be still. I've learned that healing doesn't require a crowd. Sometimes, the best thing you can do is step back, pray, and let your transformation speak louder than your explanation.

You don't have to defend your decision. You don't have to prove how hurt you were. You don't have to relive the worst moments just to be believed. God knows. And for those who truly love you, your peace is all the confirmation they need.

I do not owe full access to everyone. God sees what others don't — and that's enough. Healing quietly, is still healing. I choose peace over proving a point.

PRAYER:

Father, thank You for the gift of Your grace that protects, sustains, and transforms me. Teach me to guard it well-never taking it for granted, never using it carelessly, but living a way that reflects Your heart. May my life be a testimony that Your grace is not just received but cherished and kept. Amen

Chapter Fourteen:
Becoming Her Again —
The Woman I Lost and Found

"I praise you because I am fearfully and wonderfully made;
your works are wonderful, I know that full well."

— Psalm 139:14

There's a version of me I hadn't seen in years — strong, confident, radiant, joyful. I had buried her under years of compromise, disappointment, and emotional exhaustion. I sacrificed her to keep a marriage alive that was already on life support. But God didn't forget her. And somewhere along the way — in the silence, in the tears, in the healing — *I found her again.*

Remembering Who I Was Before the Pain

Before I became "his wife," I was God's daughter. I had dreams, laughter, creativity, and boldness. I walked with purpose, not permission. But little by little, that woman faded. With every apology I never received.

With every night I stayed up crying. With every time I forgave betrayal and ignored my own needs. Until I didn't recognize myself anymore. But healing helped me remember. And remembering helped me rise.

> *"Forget the former things; do not dwell on the past. See, I am doing a new thing!"*
> — Isaiah 43:1819

Rediscovery Is Sacred

Rediscovery doesn't mean going back to who I was — it means becoming who I was always meant to be.

I started doing the things that made my heart smile again. I danced in the kitchen. I wore colors that made me feel alive. I said no when I needed to, and yes when it aligned with my peace. I stopped settling. I stopped explaining. I stopped shrinking. God was reintroducing me to the woman He created before life tried to break her.

> *"The Lord will guide you always... You will be like a well-watered garden, like a spring whose waters never fail."*
> — Isaiah 58:11

The Mirror Doesn't Lie — It No Longer Hurts

For a long time, mirrors made me cry.

I saw disappointment. I saw failure. I saw the weight of years lost to a one-sided love.

But now? I see *strength*. I see *resilience*. I see a woman who walked through hell and came out with heaven's light in her eyes.

And I no longer need validation to feel valuable.

I smile at her. I affirm her. I fight for her.

Because she is me.

PRAYER:

Lord, thank You for not letting me stay broken. Thank You for restoring every piece of my identity and reminding me who I am in You. Help me to walk boldly in my worth and never again trade my peace for approval.

Thank You for allowing me to become the woman You designed me to be. In Jesus' name, Amen.

I am not just healing — I am becoming. I am returning to joy. I am God's masterpiece — whole, radiant, and ready.

Notes for Guidance

Chapter Fifteen:
Becoming the Woman
I Prayed to Be

*"Being confident of this, that He who began a good work in
you will carry it on to completion until the day of Christ Jesus."*
— PHILIPPIANS 1:6

There was a time when I prayed to be stronger. Wiser, Bolder.
I prayed to be the kind of woman who didn't fall apart under
pressure, who could hear God clearly, and who had peace no
matter what was going on around her.

I just didn't know that becoming her would require me to be broken
first. God didn't just answer my prayer — He processed me through
it. No one talks about how painful it is to be refined. We love the oil,
but we forget that oil only comes after the crushing. The crushing was
necessary. I thought I was strong until I had to stand alone. I thought
I was faithful until I had to trust God with everything — my money,
my mind, my future. I thought I had peace until I had to sleep through

the storm without a hand to hold. But what looked like abandonment was really alignment. God was stretching me, not punishing me. He was purging me, not forsaking me.

"Though He slay me, yet will I trust in Him..."
— Job 13:15

Becoming Her Took Obedience

Becoming the woman I prayed to be required obedience when I didn't understand.

I had to obey when I wanted revenge.

I had to obey when I felt lonely.

I had to obey when forgiveness didn't feel fair. Every time I chose God's will over my feelings, I was becoming her.

Not overnight.

But in every choice, every tear, every act of faith. I didn't realize it at the time, but every step of surrender was unlocking strength inside me that I didn't know I had.

"If you are willing and obedient,
you will eat the good things of the land."
— Isaiah 1:19

Out of all my pain came purpose. Out of all my waiting came wisdom. And out of all my faithfulness came favor I didn't see coming.

I began to walk differently.

Speak differently.

Think differently.

Not because I was pretending, but because I was finally *becoming.*

I used to pray for God to change my husband. But what He changed was me.

He taught me how to love without losing myself.

How to forgive without forgetting my worth.

How to have boundaries that didn't require bitterness.

This wasn't just healing — it was elevation.

> *"She is clothed with strength and dignity;*
> *she can laugh at the days to come."*
>
> — PROVERBS 31:25

Turning My Pain into Purpose

At this point in my journey, God had freed me from everything that was holding me back. He gave me the strength to tell my story, not for sympathy — but for *ministry.* I realized that my obedience, even when I was hurting, wasn't just for me. It was so others could be healed through my testimony.

That journey of obedience led to a new kind of boldness. I was no longer afraid to speak up. I was no longer ashamed of my story — because I knew that healing was hidden inside of it.

One day, I felt the Spirit prompting me to share my story with a woman who worked at the bank. As I began to speak, I noticed her eyes widen. She looked stunned — like I was telling *her* story. When I finished, she took a deep breath and said, "Thank you for that. My husband and I just separated, and I've been thinking about leaving Memphis."

I immediately shared with her what my spiritual mother once told me: "Don't uproot yourself for his wrongdoing. You didn't do anything wrong. Just ask God to hide him in the city, and you won't have to worry."

She listened. She prayed. And she stayed. A year later, she told me how glad she was that she hadn't moved. God had met her right where she was.

That was just one moment. Since then, God has continued to use me — not just to help women, but men too. Because men go through heartbreak. They feel rejection. They wrestle with shame. They just don't always talk about it.

God showed me that pain doesn't discriminate — and neither does healing. He was using every tear, every trial, and every testimony to reach His sons and daughters.

And now, God is using my story as a bridge for others to cross over their pain.

> *"And they overcame him by the blood of the Lamb and the word of their testimony..."*
> — REVELATION 12:11

I am not who I was — I'm who God is molding me to be.
I prayed for growth, and God gave me grace.
The woman I prayed to be is the woman I'm becoming — one obedient step at a time.

Choosing Loyalty Over Loneliness: Faithful in My Freedom

"If you love Me, keep My commandments."
— JOHN 14:15

There is something sacred about choosing loyalty when no one would fault you for doing otherwise.

After my husband walked out, I had every reason to give up — not just on marriage, but on the idea of honoring it. I was alone, hurting, and had every opportunity to take advantage of my newfound freedom.

I could've started over with someone new. I could've gone looking for attention or revenge. The world would have called it healing, empowerment, even justice. But I knew better.

I wasn't just living for people anymore — I was living for God.

I continued to wear my wedding ring, even after he left. Not because I was holding on to false hope, but because I was holding on to my vow — *the one I made before God.*

When men approached me, my answer was simple: "I'm married."

Even though I slept alone. Even though I paid the bills alone. Even though he had moved on and was enjoying the single life. I still chose to carry myself like a wife — not because I was bound to him, but because I was bound to my integrity.

"The eyes of the Lord are in every place, keeping watch on the evil and the good." — Proverbs 15:3. What good would it do me to trade in my character just to numb my loneliness? What blessing would I forfeit by choosing pleasure over purpose?

Temptation Was Real – But So Was My Faith

There were moments I wanted to stop caring. Moments when the silence was too loud. When the bed felt too big. When the reality of being alone after 15 years felt like a punishment.

But even in those moments, I felt the Spirit gently whispering, *"Stay with Me."* And I did.

I wasn't strong enough on my own. It wasn't my will power. It was the Holy Spirit inside of me that kept me anchored when everything in me wanted to drift.

Each time I said "no" to something that would have felt good in the moment but led to regret later — I saw the evidence of God's presence.

*"Walk by the Spirit, and you will not gratify
the desires of the flesh."*

— GALATIANS 5:16

This season taught me the difference between being single and being *set apart.*

God didn't just remove my husband — He created space to draw me closer to Him. I had to learn how to sleep in peace without companionship. How to fill my days without distractions. How to be okay without having to explain myself to anyone. I had to stop leaning on people for what only God could give: **comfort, security, identity, and joy.** And when I chose Him — in the quiet, in the waiting, in the tears — He showed me that He was enough. *"The Lord is near to the brokenhearted and saves the crushed in spirit."* — Psalm 34:18

It would've been easy to justify a different path. I could've said, "He left, so I'm free." Or, "He's not being faithful, why should I?" But I reminded myself — *I'm not doing this for him. I'm doing this for God.*

And when we say we love God, we can't just love His blessings — we must love His **boundaries.** *"Blessed are those who hear the word of God and obey it."* — Luke 11:28

We don't get to pick and choose which commandments are convenient. Trusting God means trusting Him completely — even when it costs you something. Even when you feel overlooked. Even when you're lonely.

Faithfulness isn't about who's watching — it's about Who you're walking with. After all, God has brought me through. How could I throw it away just to satisfy a temporary emotion? God is too good to forfeit my blessing. He gave me peace in my storm. He provided when I was unsure how the bills would be paid. He healed me in places I didn't know **I was** broken. He kept my mind when I thought

I was losing it. God has been *too good* to me for me to risk missing what He has next.

I believe every word He's spoken over my life. I believe the blessing is coming. And when it does, I want to know I remained faithful not just in church, but in my **character**.

"If ye love me, keep my commandments."

— JOHN 14:15

PRAYER:

Let us not grow weary in well doing, for in due season we shall reap, if we faint not."

— GALATIANS 6:9

Lord, thank You for giving me the strength to walk upright even when my world was falling apart. Thank You for honoring my obedience and keeping me in seasons of weakness. Help me to continue to be faithful, not for recognition, but because I love

You. I know You see my sacrifice, and I trust that nothing I surrender will be wasted. In Jesus' name, Amen.

I am faithful in my freedom. I am not moved by feelings, but led by the Spirit. I will not forfeit my future to feed my flesh. God is too good for me to settle now.

Chapter Sixteen:
Purpose in Pain — When Obedience Becomes Ministry

At some point, you realize the pain you went through wasn't just about you. It was bigger than your heartbreak, your disappointment, or your tears. God was shaping you for something deeper — ministry.

When God freed me from everything that once held me back — the fear, the shame, the loneliness — He didn't just free me to feel better. He freed me so I could speak out. So I could tell my story. So I could help other women (and even men) find healing through their hurt. God turned my obedience into a platform for others to stand on.

One day, I went to the doctor' office for a routine physical. As the nurse began preparing, I felt that familiar tug from the Holy Spirit urging me to share my testimony. At first, I hesitated, but then holy boldness rose up within me. I opened my mouth and began to share what God had done in my life.

As I spoke, tears welled up in her eyes until they began to flow. She looked at me with such heaviness, then stood and wrapped her arms around me. Through her tears she whispered, "Thank you. I needed to hear that." In that moment, I prayed for her. I could sense that the burdens she had been carrying were being lifted-not by me, but by the power of God working through me. I walked out of that office reminded that our testimonies are not meant to be kept silent. God uses them to heal, to free, and to remind others that they are not alone. That day, He reminded me that even in the most ordinary places, He can use us to do extraordinary things.

That's when it clicked: **God was using me.** Not the "me" that had it all together — but the "me" that had been through the fire. The "me" that cried in silence. That survived betrayal. That healed publicly after being broken privately.

God was using that woman — the one I used to hide.
"He comforts us in all our troubles
so that we can comfort others."
— 2 CORINTHIANS 1:4

I started to notice more and more people coming to me. Women who were quietly battling. Men who didn't know how to say they were hurting. Young adults who watched their parents' brokenness and didn't want to repeat it. And every time they came, I gave them what God gave me — truth, hope, and testimony.

Healing Is for Everyone

One thing God taught me is this: Pain doesn't have a gender. Yes, many of the women I ministered to were broken, confused, and feeling abandoned. But I saw men too. Men who needed someone to see beyond their silence. Men who were hurting from infidelity, from pride, from rejection. And they needed a safe place to be heard.

God began to use my voice to be that place. Not to judge — but to speak life.

I told them, *"God hasn't forgotten you. He's healing you too."*

So now, I walk in my purpose. Not because life is perfect — but because God used my pain for His glory. I no longer see obedience as a burden. I see it as a doorway — the very path that leads others out of their darkness.

> *"Many are the afflictions of the righteous, but the Lord delivers him out of them all."*
>
> — PSALM 34:19

Every moment of obedience… every story I share… every person I comfort — it all started with a prayer: *"Lord, use me."* And He did.

My pain has purpose.

My story is a testimony.

And my obedience is no longer just about me — it's about who's waiting on the other side of it.

PRAYER:

Father, even in the deepest valleys, You were with me. Thank You for turning my wounds into wisdom and my sorrow into a testimony. May my life always reflect that pain in Your hands becomes purpose in the lives of others. Amen

Chapter Seventeen:
Chosen for Healing

"You did not choose me, but I chose you and appointed you so that you might go and bear fruit—fruit that will last..."
— John 15:16

Sometimes I still sit in awe at how God would choose someone like me. Not because I was the strongest, not because I was the loudest, not even because I was ready — but because He knew I would obey.

I didn't feel qualified. I didn't feel prepared. I didn't even feel whole. But God saw healing in me before I could see it in myself. He chose me while I was still bleeding. He anointed me while I was still trying to make sense of the pain.

What I've learned is that God doesn't call the perfect. He perfects the called.

There is something powerful about saying "yes" to God — even when it scares you. Even when you don't know the outcome. Even when you don't think you're strong enough.

When I said yes to healing, I didn't know it would look like isolation. When I said yes to obedience, I didn't realize it would mean letting go of what I thought I needed. But every "yes" led me closer to purpose.

Every "yes" brought someone else closer to healing.

"The Spirit of the Lord is upon me... He has sent me to bind up the brokenhearted..."
— ISAIAH 61:1

Healing Isn't Always Pretty

There were days I didn't want to get out of bed. Nights I cried until my pillow was soaked. Moments when I questioned everything — my worth, my decisions, even my faith.

But healing doesn't always look graceful. Sometimes it's messy. Sometimes healing looks like showing up with tears in your eyes and worship still on your lips. Sometimes it looks like forgiveness you never thought you'd offer.

God reminded me that scars are not signs of weakness. They're signs of survival. They tell a story: *"I've been through something — but I'm still here."*

The beautiful part is that healing never left me the same. God didn't just restore me — He rebuilt me. Stronger. Wiser. More discerning.

I became the woman who knows her worth. The woman who doesn't settle. The woman who loves herself enough to walk away when peace is missing. I used to ask God, "Why me?" Now I ask, "Who else needs what I've learned?" Because healing wasn't just for me — it was meant to flow through me.

"Freely you have received; freely give."
— MATTHEW 10:8

If you're reading this, you were chosen too. You were chosen for healing. You were chosen for wholeness. You were chosen to show others that brokenness doesn't mean useless.

It just means God still has a plan.
So walk in your healing. And know this: if God could use someone like me — He can use you too.

You were never forgotten. You were always *chosen*.

PRAYER:

Thank You for choosing me, not because of my perfection, but because of Your purpose. Even in my brokenness, You saw value. Even in my pain, You saw potential. I surrender this chapter of my life to You, believing that I have been chosen for healing.

Let this be the chapter where healing begins. Let scars become testimonies. Let pain become purpose. Let every tear sown in sorrow be reaped in joy.

Chapter Eighteen:
The Glory After the Pain

"Yet what we suffer now is nothing compared to the glory He will reveal to us later."

— ROMANS 8:18

There comes a moment after the storm, after the long nights of weeping, after the soul-crushing silence — when the light finally breaks through. And you realize: you made it.

Not because it wasn't hard. Not because you didn't cry your last bit of strength away. But because God carried you through what you never thought you'd survive. And now, all that pain... has produced something beautiful.

That's the promise of God: He never wastes pain. He doesn't just bring us through the fire — He refines us *in it*. And when the refining is done, glory is revealed.

From Mourning to Dancing

There was a time I couldn't see beyond the pain. I wore my smile like armor, but inside I was shattered. I functioned broken. I served while bleeding. I smiled while grieving. I told others, "I'm fine," when I didn't even believe it myself.

But God saw through the mask. He heard the cries I couldn't speak. And little by little, moment by moment, *He healed me.*

He turned my mourning into dancing. Not all at once — but piece by piece. I didn't just wake up one day whole. I woke up one day realizing I *wasn't bleeding anymore*. Realizing that I could breathe again. That I could laugh again without guilt. That I could stand without shaking.

> *"You turned my mourning into dancing; you removed my sackcloth and clothed me with joy."*
> — PSALM 30:11

That's the kind of God we serve. One who specializes in joy after sorrow, peace after pain, glory after grief.

The Reward of Endurance

So many people see the blessing but didn't witness the battle. They see the smile, but not the struggle. They hear the testimony, but **don't see** the tears behind it. What they don't know is that the glory you carry now cost you something.

Every moment I chose *not* to give up, God was building something eternal in me.

I could've let bitterness take root. I could've chased revenge. I could've crumbled under the pressure. But instead, I chose obedience. I chose faith. I chose to trust when it didn't make sense. That's what endurance looks like. And it's not always pretty — but it's always worth it.

> *"Let us not grow weary in doing good, for at the proper time we will reap a harvest if we do not give up."*
>
> — GALATIANS 6:9

Beauty for Ashes

When I looked around at all I had lost, I thought the story was over. But God said, "Now watch what I can restore."

He didn't just give me back what I lost — He gave me more. *Better.* He gave me deeper peace. Stronger wisdom. A voice I didn't know I had. He gave me new relationships, new opportunities, new strength. He gave me *beauty for ashes.*

> *"To all who mourn… He will give a crown of beauty for ashes, a joyous blessing instead of mourning, festive praise instead of despair."*
>
> — ISAIAH 61:3

And most importantly — He gave me back. The version of me I lost in the pain. The version that knew how to love herself. That honored God with her whole life. That walked in truth without apology.

The Glory Revealed

Now when I tell my story, I don't speak from a place of pity — I speak from a place of power. Because I've seen what God can do with the broken pieces. He turned my breakdown into a breakthrough. He turned my shame into a sermon. He turned my silence into strength. I don't just see a woman who survived — I see a woman who was *made* in the fire. And every scar is a reminder:

God Brought Me Out

"For our present troubles are small and won't last very long. Yet they produce for us a glory that vastly outweighs them and will last forever."

— 2 Corinthians 4:17

So now I walk boldly. I speak freely. I love openly. And I live *knowing* that my story isn't over — it's just beginning.

If You're Still in the Pain

Let me pause and speak to the woman still in the middle of the storm. The one who doesn't see the light yet. Who's still holding back tears in front of her **children**. Who's still wondering if God really hears.

Let me tell you: *He does.*

Let me tell you: *He does.*

He sees it all. The tears. The silence. The effort it takes just to keep going. And I promise you — **glory is coming.**

Keep trusting. Keep showing up. Keep putting one foot in front of the other. Because the same God who walked me through it, is walking beside you right now.

And when you come out — and you *will* — you'll carry a glory that nothing and no one can take away. *The suffering you're going through today… is producing the strength and testimony you'll carry tomorrow."* *Hold on, Glory is on the way.*

PRAYER:

Thank You for being the God who sees, the One who never wastes our pain. As I reflect on the journey that led to this chapter, I give You all the glory-for the tears You counted, the wounds You healed, and the strength You restored.

Lord, I declare that after the pain, there shall be glory. What was meant to break me, only positioned me for purpose. What the enemy used to silence me has now become my testimony. I stand as living proof that You are a Redeemer, a Restorer, and a Rewarder of those who diligently seek You.

Notes for Guidance

Chapter Nineteen:
To the Broken Woman —
This is Not the End of You

"The Lord is close to the brokenhearted and saves those who are crushed in spirit."

— Psalm 34:18

To every woman reading this with tears in her eyes, wondering how much more she can take — I see you. And more importantly, **God sees you**.

This chapter is for you — the woman who feels like the life she built is crumbling. The wife who just found out her husband has been unfaithful. The woman drowning in shame, trying to hold her head up while silently falling apart. The one going through a divorce she never imagined would happen. The woman who's allowing her husband to walk all over her — not because she's weak, but because she loves too deeply and **has forgotten** her own worth.

Let me say this to you clearly and boldly: **being broken should not leave you in pieces**.

You Are Not What Happened To You

You are not the affair. You are not the rejection. You are not the mistake, the heartbreak, or the failure. You are still God's daughter. Still chosen. Still worthy. Still powerful.

Yes, you may feel like you're barely holding on. But I need you to know that **your identity has not changed — your circumstances did**.

God is still with you. Still for you. Still writing a story that will bring Him glory — even from this place.

Divorce Is a Chapter, Not the Whole Book

If you're facing a divorce, I want you to breathe. Deeply. Because although this hurts deeply — it does not end up with you. Divorce may be the death of a marriage, but it's *not* the death of you. You still have a purpose. You still have a future. God can still bring healing, restoration, and joy into your life. Don't let the enemy convince you that one failed chapter means a failed life. There were moments while writing this book when I found myself torn – confused about whether to move forward with a divorce or simply wait and trust the process. The truth is, even as I write these words, I'm still not fully certain. But what I do know is this: God is not finished with my story. Maybe part two of this journey will be the testimony of what God had planned for my life all along. Until then, I'm trusting him- one page at a time.

"Behold, I will do a new thing; now it shall spring forth."

— Isaiah 43:19

To the Woman Being Walked On

To the woman letting her husband walk all over her because she's trying to "keep the peace" — please hear me:

Peace that costs your dignity is not peace.

You were never called to be a doormat. Submission is not slavery. Love is not abuse. Marriage is not supposed to destroy you — it's meant to reflect God's love.

If you've lost yourself while trying to save your marriage, it's time to ask God to help you find *you* again.

To the Woman Who Just Found Out

That kind of betrayal is the kind that hits you in the chest. It makes you question everything — your beauty, your worth, your memories, your sanity.

But I need you to understand something: **his cheating is not a reflection of your value.**

It's a reflection of his choices. His brokenness. His lack of integrity. You do not become less valuable because someone failed to honor you. You are still fearfully and wonderfully made. You are still enough. Let the tears fall. Let the questions come. But don't let this break you.

Don't Let Broken Turn In Pieces

Yes, you are broken right now. But brokenness in the hands of God becomes transformation. This is not the end of your story. This is the *becoming.*

You are becoming wiser. Stronger. More discerning. You are learning to love yourself again. To choose peace over pleasing. To choose healing over hiding.

"He heals the brokenhearted and binds up their wounds."
— PSALM 147:3

You don't have to fall apart quietly. You don't have to walk in shame. Speak up. Stand up. Get help. Get healing. Because you deserve to be whole again.

A Final Word to You

God is near. He sees your tears. He heard your cry last night. And He is still the God who restores. You are not alone. You are not crazy. You are not too far gone.

You are simply in a season of refining. And when this is over — you will rise. Not just back to who you were — but to who you were always meant to be. **This is not the end of you. It's just the beginning of something new.**

PRAYER:

Father, I lift up every woman who feels shattered, overlooked, or forgotten. You see every tear she's cried in the dark, and You hold every piece of her heart in the palm of Your hand. Remind her that her brokenness does not disqualify her-it is the place where Your healing begins. Speak life into the places that feel dead, hope into the places that feel empty, and strength into the places that feel weak.

Lord, cover her in Your unfailing love. Let her know she is still chosen, still worthy, and still called. Restore her joy, renew her mind, and give her the courage to believe again. Turn her pain into power, her wounds into wisdom, and her story into a song of victory. In Jesus' name, Amen.

Notes for Guidance

Chapter Twenty:
Final Healing —
Letting God Finish the Work

*"Create in me a clean heart, O God,
and renew a right spirit within me."*
— Psalm 51:10

This is the final chapter —
but not the end of your story.

*It's the part where you stop pretending and start healing
from the inside out. The part where you stop running from
the pain and instead ask God to meet you in it. The part
where you invite Him into the places you've hidden — the
bitterness, the rage, the fear, the disappointment — and say,
"God, I don't want to carry this anymore."*

Don't Let Anger Become Hate

You have every right to be angry. You were hurt. Betrayed. Mistreated. Lied to. Disrespected. But let me tell you something: **anger that is not surrendered to God will become poison to your soul**. It will eat away at your peace, cloud your judgment, and keep you tied to what hurt you. The Bible says, *"Be angry and do not sin; do not let the sun go down on your anger."* (Ephesians 4:26) Anger in itself is not a sin. But hate is. Resentment is. Bitterness is. And the longer you hold onto anger without releasing it to God, the more you give the enemy space to build strongholds in your heart.

You cannot move on while secretly wishing pain on the person who hurt you. You cannot be free while holding your ex hostage in your mind.

Let it go. Give it to God. Forgiveness isn't saying what they did was okay. It's saying *you refuse to let it control you anymore.*

You Have to Face What's In Your Heart

Real healing doesn't happen by ignoring the pain. It happens when you face it. When you sit in the silence and allow God to expose what's really in your heart:

The jealousy
The rage
The insecurity
The need for revenge

Ask yourself: *Have I really released this? Have I truly forgiven? Or am I just masking it?*

We serve a God who wants to heal us completely — but He can't heal what we pretend doesn't exist. You've got to be honest. Cry if you need to. Scream if you must. Journal it. Pray it. Bring it to the altar.

Because the only way out — is *through.*

"Search me, God, and know my heart... See if there is any offensive way in me, and lead me in the way everlasting."
— Psalm 139:23-24

Be Careful Who You Share With

Everyone is not called to counsel you. Be mindful of who you're sharing your pain with.

Some people feed it instead of helping you heal from it. Some offer advice rooted in bitterness or trauma, not wisdom.

The Bible says, *"In the multitude of counselors there is safety,"* (Proverbs 11:14) — but that *only* applies when those counselors are wise, Spirit-led, and grounded in truth.

You need **spiritual guidance** — someone who can pray you through when you can't pray for yourself. And in some cases, you need **professional therapy** too. There is no shame in seeking help. Sometimes, what's broken in us is layered — and it takes time and expertise to unpack.

Healing is not always instant. But it's always worth it.

When the Answer Doesn't Come — Seek the Scriptures

There will be days when even the best advice won't answer your questions. When your spirit is still restless. That's when you turn to the Word.

Open your Bible and ask God to show you what to do. Don't just search for a verse to match your feelings — search for God's heart.

His Word is alive. It corrects. It comforts. It clarifies.

And it still speaks today.

When you feel lost, pray:

"Lord, order my steps in Your Word. Light my path. Speak clearly. I want to do this Your way." And trust that He will.

"Your word is a lamp to my feet and a light to my path."
— Psalm 119:105

When He's Willing – Consider Carefully

Now I must speak to the woman with a husband who is *willing* —
not perfect, not fixed overnight, but willing to change and surrender
to God.

Before you walk away from a marriage, ask yourself: *Is he finally
becoming the man I prayed for?*

Sometimes, what we prayed for shows up in a form we didn't
expect. Sometimes, the breakthrough comes right after the breaking.
And if your husband is humbling himself, seeking God, going to coun-
seling, confessing and repenting — don't rush out the door.

That kind of surrender is rare. Don't let your pain blind you to the
fact that God may be answering your prayer — just not in the way
you imagined. Pray for discernment. Don't ignore red flags. But don't
ignore growth either.

*"A wise woman builds her house, but with her own hands the
foolish one tears hers down."*
— Proverbs 14:1

Final Word: Let God Finish the Work

This chapter may be the last in this book — but it's the beginning
of your next chapter with God.

Let Him finish the healing. Let Him renew your heart. Let Him
guide your steps. Let Him restore what was lost — or give you something brand new. You've come too far to go back now.

You've cried too many tears to not walk into wholeness.

You've survived too much to live beneath your worth.

Let God complete what He started. Because when He heals you fully — you'll never be the same.

> *"Being confident of this very thing,*
> *that He who has begun a good work in you will complete it..."*
> — PHILIPPIANS 1:6

This is your time. This is your healing. This is your new beginning.

Notes for Guidance

A Closing Prayer

Father God,

Thank You for every woman who has walked through these pages with tears in her eyes and hope in her heart. Thank You for meeting us in our brokenness, for showing up when we were too weak to stand, and for speaking life into dead places.

I pray that she finds peace — not just the peace that silences the noise, but the kind that restores her soul. I pray that she heard Your voice through every chapter, through every testimony, through every word. Lord, help her to heal the right way. Help her to face what's been buried and surrender what she cannot fix. Help her release anger before it turns to hate, and guide her toward wise counsel, sound wisdom, and truth.

Show her what love really looks like again — starting with Your love.

Father, if her husband is willing and surrendering to You, give her discernment to see growth and wisdom to choose restoration over reaction.

Remind her that she is not forgotten. That her story is not over. That her life still carries purpose.

Thank You for being a God who brings beauty from ashes. In Jesus' name, **Amen.**

I pray that you found some kind of peace in your hurt, and that you were able to hear God through the pages.

The Author

Monica D. Brazell is a woman of faith, resilience, and purpose. After enduring a 15-year marriage marked by betrayal, emotional abuse, and heartbreak, she made the courageous choice to surrender her pain to God and walk into healing. Through prayer, obedience, and the unwavering support of her spiritual community, Monica found her voice — and now uses it to help other women find theirs.

She is a proud mother of three and grandmother to two beautiful children who inspire her every day to live boldly and love deeply. Monica is committed to helping women navigate brokenness without falling to pieces — encouraging them to trust God through every chapter of life.

Broken but Not in Pieces is her debut book — a testimony of pain transformed into purpose and proof that God still restores.

www.ingramcontent.com/pod-product-compliance
Lightning Source LLC
Chambersburg PA
CBHW072200090426
42740CB00012B/2330